TRADITIONAL SONGS

I've Been Working on the Railroad

Edited by Ann Owen   Illustrated by Sandra D'Antonio

Music Consultant: Peter Mercer-Taylor, Ph.D., Associate Professor of Musicology,
University of Minnesota, Minneapolis, Minnesota

Reading Consultant: Susan Kesselring, M.A., Literacy Educator
Rosemount-Apple Valley-Eagan (Minnesota) School District

DINAH'S PLACE

PICTURE WINDOW BOOKS
MINNEAPOLIS, MINNESOTA

Traditional Songs series editor: Peggy Henrikson
Page production: The Design Lab
Musical arrangement: Elizabeth Temple
The illustrations in this book were rendered in pen with digital coloring.

PICTURE WINDOW BOOKS
151 Good Counsel Drive
P.O. Box 669
Mankato, MN 56002-0669
1-877-845-8392
www.picturewindowbooks.com

Printed in the United States of America.

Library of Congress Cataloging-in-Publication Data

I've been working on the railroad / edited by Ann Owen ; illustrated by Sandra D'Antonio.
p. cm. — (Traditional songs)
Summary: Presents an illustrated version of the traditional song along with some discussion
of its folk origins.
Includes bibliographical references (p.).
ISBN-13: 978-1-4048-0151-6 (hardcover)
ISBN-10: 1-4048-0151-0 (hardcover)
ISBN-13: 978-1-4048-0431-9 (softcover)
ISBN-10: 1-4048-0431-5 (softcover)
1. Folk songs, English—United States—History and criticism—Juvenile literature.
2. Railroads—Songs and music—History and criticism—Juvenile literature. 3. Children's
songs—Texts. [1. Railroads—Songs and music. 2. Songs.] I. Owen, Ann, 1953–
II. D'Antonio, Sandra, 1956– ill. III. Series.
ML3551 .I83 2003
782.42162'13'00268—dc21
2002155298

What do you see when you sing a song? Does the music come in colors?

What do you do when you sing a song? Does the melody make you dance?

What do you hear when you sing a song? Do the words tell a story?

Let's explore the sights and sounds of one of our favorite songs.

Who's been working on the railroad?

I've been working
on the railroad,
all the live long day.

I've been working on the railroad,
just to pass the time away.

Dinah, won't you blow,
Dinah, won't you blow,
Dinah, won't you
blow your horn?

Dinah, won't you blow,
Dinah, won't you blow,
Dinah, won't you blow your horn?

Someone's in the kitchen
with Dinah.

Someone's in the kitchen, I know.
Someone's in the kitchen with Dinah,
strumming on the old banjo.

And singing,
"Fee, fie, fiddle-i-o,
fee, fie, fiddle-i-o,
fee, fie, fiddle-i-o,"

strumming on the old banjo.

I've Been Working on the Railroad

I've been working on the railroad, all the live long day.

I've been working on the railroad, just to pass the time away.

Can't you hear the whistle blowing? Rise up so early in the morn.

Can't you hear the captain shouting, "Dinah, blow your horn!"

Dinah, won't you blow, Dinah, won't you blow, Dinah, won't you blow your

horn? Dinah, won't you blow, Dinah, won't you blow,

Dinah, won't you blow your horn? Some-one's in the kitchen with Dinah.

Some-one's in the kitchen, I know. Some-one's in the kitchen with Dinah,

strumming on the old banjo. And singing, "Fee, fie, fiddle-i-o,

fee, fie, fiddle-i-o. fee, fie,

fiddle-i-o," strumming on the old banjo.

About the Song

Many songs have been written about trains and the railroad. "I've Been Working on the Railroad" is perhaps the best known. Some people think it came from an African-American song sung by men working on riverboats. Others believe the melody is from an old hymn. They think the men who laid the miles and miles of railroad track across the country gave the song new words. The men sang as they worked. Later, the parts "Dinah won't you blow" and "Someone's in the kitchen with Dinah" were added to the song. Dinah is either a woman or a train engine. Blowing her horn is the call to lunch.

DID YOU KNOW?

Over 20,000 men worked in the crews that laid the tracks for the first railroad line across the United States. The line was completed in 1869. "I've Been Working on the Railroad" became popular in the late 1800s. By then, crews had laid about 190,000 miles (305,700 kilometers) of track. Railroad travel was the greatest in the United States in 1916. At that time, over 254,000 miles (408,700 kilometers) of track had been laid.

Make a Musical Instrument: Banjo Box

WHAT YOU NEED:

- shoe box with lid (or an empty tissue box)
- scissors
- brown paper or construction paper
- crayons or markers
- glue or tape
- 5 rubber bands (different sizes)
- an adult to help you

WHAT TO DO:

1. Have an adult help you cut a round hole in the lid of the box, unless you are using a tissue box, which already has a hole.
2. Cover the box (and lid) with paper, wrapping it so the hole is still open. Glue or tape the paper down.
3. Decorate the paper on your box with crayons or markers.
4. Place the lid back on the box. Put the rubber bands around the box the short way, crossing them over the hole.
5. You're ready to play your banjo box!

To Learn More

AT THE LIBRARY

Cohn, Amy L. *From Sea to Shining Sea: a Treasury of American Folklore and Folk Songs*. New York: Scholastic, 1993.

Keats, Ezra Jack. *John Henry, an American Legend*. New York: Alfred A. Knopf, 1987.

Krull, Kathleen. *Gonna Sing My Head Off!: American Folk Songs for Children*. New York: Alfred A. Knopf, 1992.

Stille, Darlene R. *Freight Trains*. Minneapolis: Compass Point Books, 2002.

Yolen, Jane. *Jane Yolen's Old MacDonald Songbook*. Honesdale, Pa.: Boyds Mills Press, 1994.

ON THE WEB

CHILDREN'S MUSIC WEB
http://www.childrensmusic.org
For resources and links on children's music for kids, parents, educators, and musicians

NATIONAL INSTITUTE OF ENVIRONMENTAL HEALTH SCIENCES KIDS' PAGES: CHILDREN'S SING-ALONG SONGS
http://www.niehs.nih.gov/kids/musicchild.htm
For music and lyrics to many favorite, traditional children's songs

FACT HOUND
Want more information about traditional songs? FACT HOUND offers a safe, fun way to find Web sites. All of the sites on Fact Hound have been researched by our staff. Simply follow these steps:

1. Visit *http://www.facthound.com*.
2. Enter a search word or 1404801510.
3. Click Fetch It.

Your trusty Fact Hound will fetch the best sites for you!